Macmillan/McGraw-Hill **TIMELINKS**

People and Places

PROGRAM AUTHORS

James A. Banks
Kevin P. Colleary
Linda Greenow
Walter C. Parker
Emily M. Schell
Dinah Zike

CONTRIBUTORS

Raymond C. Jones
Irma M. Olmedo

Mc Graw Hill **Macmillan/McGraw-Hill**

Citizenship

PROGRAM AUTHORS

James A. Banks, Ph.D.
Kerry and Linda Killinger Professor
  of Diversity Studies and Director, Center
  for Multicultural Education
University of Washington
Seattle, Washington

Kevin P. Colleary, Ed.D.
Curriculum and Teaching Department
Graduate School of Education
Fordham University
New York, New York

Linda Greenow, Ph.D.
Associate Professor and Chair
Department of Geography
State University of New York at New Paltz
New Paltz, New York

Walter C. Parker, Ph.D.
Professor of Social Studies Education,
  Adjunct Professor of Political Science
University of Washington
Seattle, Washington

Emily M. Schell, Ed.D.
Visiting Professor, Teacher Education
San Diego State University
San Diego, California

Dinah Zike
Educational Consultant
Dinah-Mite Activities, Inc.
San Antonio, Texas

CONTRIBUTORS

Raymond C. Jones, Ph.D.
Director of Secondary Social Studies
  Education
Wake Forest University
Winston-Salem, North Carolina

Irma M. Olmedo
Associate Professor
University of Illinois-Chicago
College of Education
Chicago, Illinois

GRADE LEVEL REVIEWERS

Kathleen Clark
Second Grade Teacher
Edison Elementary
Fraser, Michigan

Patricia Hinchliff
Second Grade Teacher
West Woods School
Hamden, Connecticut

Pamela South
Second Grade Teacher
Greenwood Elementary School
Princess Anne, Maryland

Karen Starr
Second Grade Teacher
Arthur Froberg Elementary School
Rockford, Illinois

EDITORIAL ADVISORY BOARD

Bradley R. Bakle
Assistant Superintendent
East Allen County Schools
New Haven, Indiana

Marilyn Barr
Assistant Superintendent for Instruction
Clyde-Savannah Central School
Clyde, New York

Lisa Bogle
Elementary Coordinator, K-5
Rutherford County Schools
Murfreesboro, Tennessee

Janice Buselt
Campus Support, Primary and ESOL
Wichita Public Schools
Wichita, Kansas

Kathy Cassioppi
Social Studies Coordinator
Rockford Public Schools, District 205
Rockford, Illinois

Denise Johnson, Ph.D.
Social Studies Supervisor
Knox County Schools
Knoxville, Tennessee

Steven Klein, Ph.D.
Social Studies Coordinator
Illinois School District U-46
Elgin, Illinois

Sondra Markman
Curriculum Director
Warren Township Board of Education
Warren Township, New Jersey

Cathy Nelson
Social Studies Coordinator
Columbus Public Schools
Columbus, Ohio

Holly Pies
Social Studies Coordinator
Vigo County Schools
Terre Haute, Indiana

Avon Ruffin
Social Studies County Supervisor
Winston-Salem/Forsyth Schools
Lewisville, North Carolina

Chuck Schierloh
Social Studies Curriculum Team Leader
Lima City Schools
Lima, Ohio

Bob Shamy
Social Studies Supervisor
East Brunswick Public Schools
East Brunswick, New Jersey

Judy Trujillo
Social Studies Coordinator
Columbia Missouri School District
Columbia, Missouri

Gayle Voyles
Director of the Center for Economic
  Education
Kansas City School District
Kansas City, Missouri

Todd Wigginton
Coordinator of Social Studies K-12
Metropolitan Nashville Public Schools
Nashville, Tennessee

RFB&D 🎧
learning through listening

Students with print disabilities may be eligible to obtain an accessible, audio version of the pupil edition of this textbook. Please call Recording for the Blind & Dyslexic at 1-800-221-4792 for complete information.

The **McGraw·Hill** Companies

Macmillan McGraw-Hill

MHID 0-02-152403-3   ISBN 978-0-02-152403-7   Printed in the United States of America

6 7 8 9 10 QVR/LEH 13 12

People and Places

Table of Contents

Skills and Features

Map and Globe Skills

Chart and Graph Skills

People, Places, and Events

Maps

How Government Works

People, Places, and Events

Judges

These **judges** work to keep our laws fair.

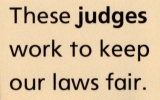

The **Supreme Court** is the place where the judges work.

Supreme Court

A Judge Is Appointed

Samuel Alito was **appointed**
by the President to be a
judge on the Supreme Court.

3

We the People

Vocabulary

government

Constitution

election

Reading Skill

Cause and Effect

Cause		Effect
	→	

4

Our Government

Government helps big groups of people get along. A government is all of the people who run a community, state, or country. Government workers meet to find ways to make our lives better.

 What is government?

Government workers talk about a new law.

Our first leaders plan the Constitution.

Our Constitution

Our country's first leaders worked hard to plan a good government. They wanted a fair government that would keep people safe and free.

The plan they wrote is called the **Constitution**. The Constitution says that our government is run by its citizens.

The Constitution says that we choose our own leaders. It says that each state helps to decide on our laws. It also says that we are free to say and write what we think. It says that we are free to choose our religion.

 What are three things our Constitution says?

Event
Signing the Constitution

Leaders from 12 states met on September 17, 1787. They took turns signing the Constitution. Today, we still follow our Constitution.

Citizens Rule

One way citizens rule our government is by voting. Citizens vote to choose our leaders and lawmakers. Citizens also vote to choose new laws. The special time when citizens vote is called an **election**.

By voting, citizens control government. So, we say that the United States government is of the people, by the people, and for the people.

 How do citizens rule our country?

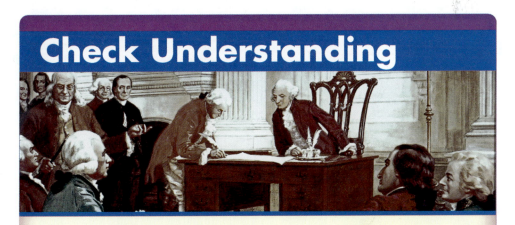

Check Understanding

1. **Vocabulary** What is an <mark>election</mark>?

2. **Cause and Effect** How are government leaders chosen?

Cause	Effect

3. How does government help us?

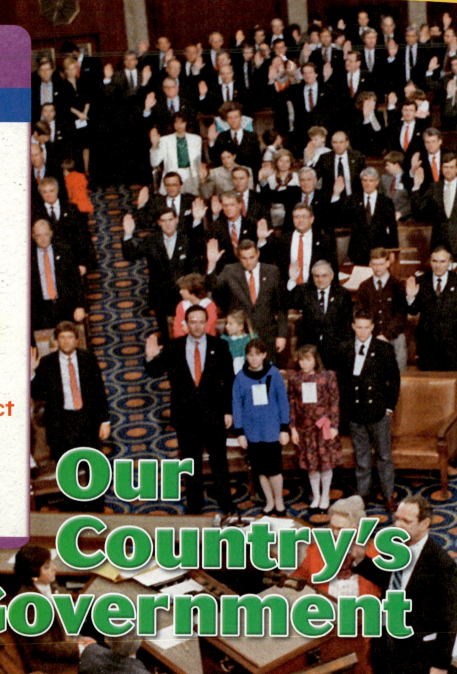

Lesson 2

Vocabulary

judge

Congress

court

Supreme Court

Reading Skill

Cause and Effect

Cause	Effect

Our Country's Government

Three Parts of Government

Our government is divided into three parts. Each part is run by a different group of people. The three groups are leaders, lawmakers, and **judges**. A judge is the person who decides what our laws mean.

Our Constitution says that our leaders, lawmakers, and judges must work together. That way, one part of our government will not have too much power.

 What three groups run our government?

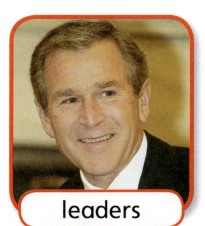

leaders

lawmakers

The Three Parts of Government

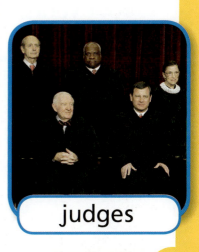

judges

Our Leaders, Our Lawmakers

The President is the leader of our country. The President's job is to make sure everyone follows the laws of our country. He works with leaders from other countries, too. We vote to choose our President once every four years.

Around the World

Great Britain is a country in Europe. It was once ruled by kings and queens. Today, the leader of Great Britain is called the prime minister.

Congress

All of our country's lawmakers together are called **Congress**. Congress makes laws for the people of our country. First, lawmakers talk and write about an idea for a new law. Then, Congress votes "yes" or "no" to decide if the idea should become a law.

 What is the President's job?

Our Judges

Judges work in a place called a **court**. The most important court in our country is the **Supreme Court**. It is in Washington, D.C. Judges in the Supreme Court make sure that our laws agree with our Constitution.

In a court, a judge decides what is fair. A judge decides if a person has broken a law. If the person has broken a law, the judge may decide on a punishment.

 What is a judge's job?

Check Understanding

1. **Vocabulary** What is a **court**?

2. **Cause and Effect** What happens after Congress talks and writes about an idea for a law?

Cause	Effect

3. Why do the three parts of our government work together?

Citizenship

Points of View

What makes a good leader?

These second graders are from Little Rock, Arkansas. Read about what they think makes a person a good leader.

Little Rock, Arkansas

"A good leader can solve problems by talking about things. A leader helps others, and makes good decisions, and is honest. She protects others from danger."

Maria Meneses Ramos

Maria Meneses Ramos

"A good leader directs others in what to do and explains plans. A good leader is someone who cares about what happens to people all around the world."

Diana Basnakian

Diana Basnakian

"A good leader helps other people overcome their fears. My cousin is a good leader. When I was little, I was scared of dogs, but he gave me a puppy and showed me how it wasn't scary."

Keito Alexander

Keito Alexander

Vocabulary

capital

Capitol

diagram

monument

Reading Skill

Cause and Effect

Cause		Effect
	→	

Our Country's Capital

Washington, D.C.

The city of Washington, D.C., belongs to all people in the United States. It is called the ==capital== of the United States. A capital city is where government workers work.

Washington, D.C., has many important buildings. The ==Capitol== building is where Congress makes laws for our country.

What is a capital city?

The White House

The White House is the building where the President lives and works. The White House has many rooms.

The **diagram** on the next page shows the inside of the White House. A diagram is a picture that shows the parts of something.

The White House

1 **State Dining Room** The President and guests eat dinner here.

2 **Red Room** First Lady Eleanor Roosevelt met news reporters here.

3 **Blue Room** President Grover Cleveland got married in this room.

4 **Green Room** President James Monroe liked to play cards here.

5 **East Room** This is the largest room in the White House. It is used for concerts, dances, and large meetings.

 Which is the largest room in the White House? How is the room used?

Monuments

There are many **monuments** in Washington, D.C. A monument is a building or statue that shows special respect for a person or event. The Washington Monument shows respect for our first President.

The Jefferson Memorial shows our respect for our third President, Thomas Jefferson. He wrote the Declaration of Independence.

Jefferson
Memorial

Washington
Monument

Abraham Lincoln was one of our greatest Presidents. A monument called the Lincoln Memorial helps us remember how he cared about freedom for all.

 Can you name three Presidents?

Lincoln Memorial

Check Understanding

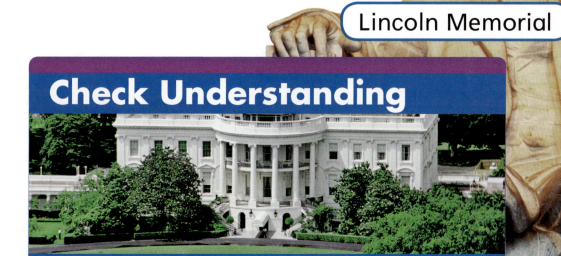

1. **Vocabulary** What is the <mark>Capitol</mark> building?

2. **Cause and Effect** Why do people build monuments?

Cause	Effect

3. **EXPLORE The Big Idea** Why is Washington, D.C., an important city?

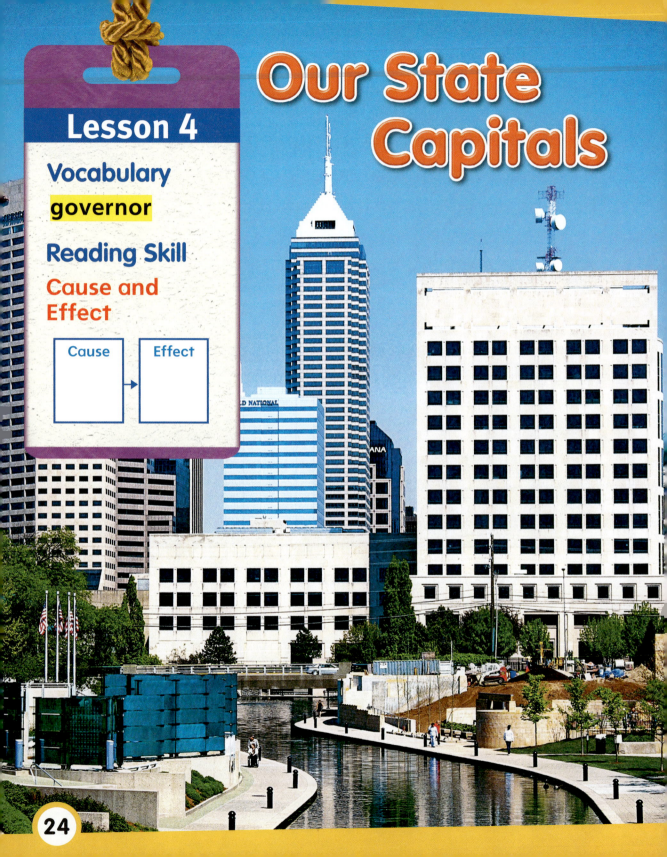

Our State Capitals

Vocabulary

governor

Reading Skill

Cause and Effect

Cause		Effect
	→	

Capital Cities

Each of our 50 states has its own capital city. For example, Indianapolis is the capital city of Indiana.

Every capital city has its own capitol building. State government workers work in the capitol building that is located in their capital city.

 **What is your state's capital city?**

Indiana State Capitol building in Indianapolis

State Government

Each state has a government with three parts. Like the government of our country, each state has a leader, lawmakers, and judges.

The leader of a state is called the **governor**. Citizens of a state vote for the governor and state lawmakers.

Deval Patrick is the governor of Massachusetts.

Places
Boston's Capitol Building

Boston is the capital city of the state of Massachusetts. This is Boston's capitol building. It is where Governor Deval Patrick works.

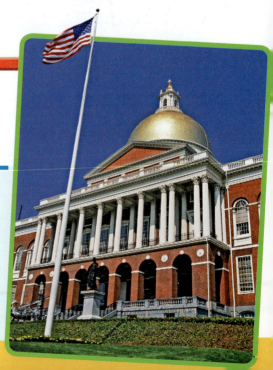

The Supreme Court of Ohio has seven judges.

Each state has a state supreme court.
Each state also has its own constitution.
The judges follow the state constitution
to make sure the state laws are fair.

 How is state government like the government of our country?

State Symbols

You know that our country's flag belongs to everyone. But, did you know that each state has its own flag, too? Ohio's state flag has a blue triangle that stands for hills and valleys. The circle stands for the "O" in the word Ohio.

Our country's flower is the red rose. Our country's bird is the bald eagle. Each state has its own bird and flower, too. New Jersey's state flower is the violet.

violet

Ohio's flag

Indiana's state bird is the cardinal. What is your state's flower and bird?

 What kinds of symbols does your state have?

cardinal

Check Understanding

1. **Vocabulary** What is a <mark>governor</mark>?

2. **Cause and Effect** How is the state governor chosen?

Cause	Effect

3. Where do state leaders, lawmakers, and judges work?

Use a Compass Rose

Look at the symbol below. It is called a **compass rose**. A compass rose has arrows that point to the letters **N**, **S**, **E**, and **W**. These arrows show the directions north, south, east, and west.

Look at the map of Ohio.
Can you find the compass rose?

Places to Visit in Ohio

Lake Erie

North
West · East
South

Map Scale
0   20   40 miles

Miami River

Scioto River

Ohio River

Map Key
- Toledo Zoo
- Cleveland Botanical Garden
- Ohio State Capitol
- Wagner National Forest
- Serpent Mound

Try the Skill

1. What is a **compass rose**?

2. Is Serpent Mound north or south of the Ohio State Capitol?

Writing Activity
Write the directions to go from Toledo Zoo to Cleveland Botanical Gardens.

Vocabulary

<mark>mayor</mark>

Reading Skill

Cause and Effect

Cause	Effect

Community Government

Community Leaders

Community government is also made up of three parts. Leaders, lawmakers, and judges in a city work in a building called city hall.

In many communities, the leader is called the **mayor**. A mayor makes sure that community laws are followed. Mark Funkhouser is the mayor of Kansas City, Missouri.

 Who works at city hall?

Mayor Mark Funkhouser

The city council of Kansas City, Missouri

CITY OF FOUNTAINS
HEART OF THE NATION

KANSAS CITY
MISSOURI

Lawmakers and Judges

Community lawmakers meet to make laws and solve problems for the community. In Kansas City, Missouri, this group of lawmakers is called the city council.

In Kansas City, if you break a law you may have to go to a community court. For example, littering is against the law in Kansas City. A person who litters might have to go to a court and see a judge.

 What is the group of lawmakers in Kansas City called?

Check Understanding

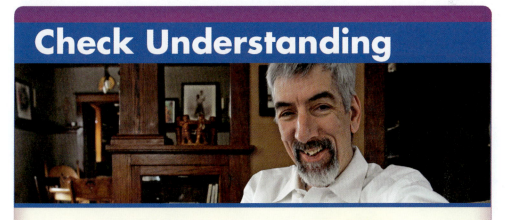

1. **Vocabulary** What is a <mark>mayor</mark>?

2. **Cause and Effect** Why might a person have to see a judge?

Cause	Effect

3. 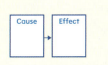 Why does the city council meet?

Vocabulary

justice

immigrant

Reading Skill

Cause and Effect

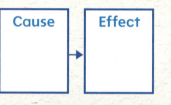

Cause		Effect

Justice for All

The Pledge of Allegiance

Our flag stands for freedom and <mark>justice</mark>. Justice means fairness. We make a promise to be loyal to our country when we say the Pledge of Allegiance to our flag.

Pledge of Allegiance

I pledge allegiance to the flag of the United States of America and to the republic for which it stands, one Nation under God, indivisible, with liberty and justice for all.

 What does our flag stand for?

Coming to America

America is a nation of **immigrants**. An immigrant is a person who leaves one country to live in another.

Long ago most immigrants sailed to America on ships. They could see the Statue of Liberty when they arrived at Ellis Island in New York. The Statue of Liberty stands for freedom.

Statue of Liberty

Millions of immigrants from around the world have come to live in America. Today people still come to make America their home. Some come to live in freedom. Others come to make a better life.

 What are some reasons that people come to America?

These immigrants are becoming American citizens.

Working for Justice

America has a tradition of working hard for freedom and fairness. Years ago women in our country were not allowed to vote. Elizabeth Cady Stanton and Susan B. Anthony knew that this was not fair.

Susan B. Anthony and Elizabeth Cady Stanton

Anthony talked to lawmakers in Congress. Stanton and Anthony wrote a newspaper. They led marches. They worked hard for a new law that allowed women to vote.

Today all citizens over age 18 can vote. Our country became more fair because of these women.

How did Stanton and Anthony work for justice?

The law changed in 1920. Women could vote! ▶

Rosa Parks

Leaders for Justice

Rosa Parks was a leader for justice. One unfair law said that black people had to give up their seats to white people on buses. Parks would not give up her seat to a white person. Police took her to jail.

People
Dr. Martin Luther King, Jr.

Dr. Martin Luther King, Jr., was a leader for justice. He said, "Injustice anywhere is a threat to justice everywhere."

Dr. Martin Luther King, Jr., helped Rosa Parks. He told people to stop riding buses until the unfair bus law was changed. The United States government listened when Parks and King stood up for justice.

 How did Martin Luther King, Jr., help?

Check Understanding

1. **Vocabulary** What is justice?

2. **Cause and Effect** How did Rosa Parks help to change a law?

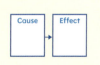

Cause	Effect

3.  What things can people do to change unfair laws?

Vocabulary

Number a paper from I to 3. Next to each number write the word that matches the meaning.

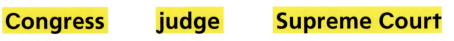

Congress   **judge**   **Supreme Court**

1. a person who decides if a law was broken

2. lawmakers who work in Washington, D.C.

3. the most important court in our country

Critical Thinking

4. Who do you know who would be a good leader? Why?

5. How is the United States government like state government?

Skill

Use a Compass Rose

Look at the compass rose and map.
Answer the question below.

Places to Visit in Washington, D.C.

Map Scale
0   1,000   2,000 feet

E Street

Constitution Avenue

North

West — East

South

Pennsylvania Avenue

14th Street

Independence Avenue

Potomac River

Tidal Basin

Map Key

White House

Lincoln Memorial

Washington Monument

U.S. Capitol

6. In which direction do you travel to get from the U.S. Capitol to the Lincoln Memorial?

A. north

B. south

C. east

D. west

Government Activity

Make a Symbols Mobile

1. Draw and label pictures of our country's flag, bird, and flower on index cards.

2. Find out about your own state's flag, bird, and flower.

3. On the back of the three index cards, draw and label your own state's flag, bird, and flower.

4. Attach the pictures to a coat hanger.

Ruffed Grouse

Mountain Laurel

Flag

Picture Glossary

C

capital The city where the people of our government work. *Indianopolis is the **capital** city of Indiana.* (page 19)

Capitol The building where lawmakers work. *The **Capitol** building is located in Washington, D.C.* (page 19)

compass rose A symbol on a map that has arrows that point out the directions north, east, south, and west. *The **compass rose** helped us find our way south from the Toledo Zoo to the Ohio State Capitol.* (page 30)

Congress All of our country's lawmakers together. *We saw where **Congress** works when we visited Washington, D.C.* (page 13)

Constitution The plan for our government. *The **Constitution** says that we are free to say and write what we think.* (page 6)

court A place where judges work. *This **court** is located in St. Louis, Missouri.* (page 14)

D

diagram A picture with labels to tell what things are. *This **diagram** shows the different parts of the White House.* (page 20)

E

election The special time when we vote for our leaders and new laws. *We had an **election** to vote for a President.* (page 8)

G

government The group of people who lead a community, state, or country. ***Government** workers meet to find ways to make our lives better.* (page 5)

governor The leader of a state. *The citizens of Massachusetts elected Deval Patrick to be the new **governor**.* (page 26)

I

immigrant A person who leaves one country to live in another. *My great grandmother was an **immigrant** from Ireland.* (page 38)

J

judge A person who decides what the laws mean. ***Judges** make sure that laws are fair.* (page II)

justice Fairness. *Susan B. Anthony cared about justice for all women.* (page 37)

M

mayor The leader of a community. *Mark Funkhouser is the mayor of Kansas City, Missouri.* (page 33)

monument A building or a statue that shows special respect for a person or event. *The Washington Monument shows respect for our first President.* (page 22)

S

Supreme Court The most important court in our country. *The Supreme Court is located in Washington, D.C.* (page 14)

Index

This index lists many things you can find in your book. It tells the page numbers on which they are found. If you see the letter *m* before a page number, you will find a map on that page.

Credits

Maps: XNR

Illustrations:
9: Remy Simard. 16-17: Hector Borlasca.

Photography Credits: All Photographs are by Macmillan/McGraw-hill (MMH) except as noted below.

1: William S Helsel/Getty Images. 2: (br) Tom Brakefield/Getty Images; (cl) Matthew Cavanaugh/epa/CORBIS; (cr) Siede Preis/Getty Images. 3: (br) Jacqueline Mia Foster/PhotoEdit; (c) Pablo Martinez Monsivais, Pool/AP Photos. 4: R.Nowitz/Photri-Microstock. 5: (b) Getty Images. 6: (t) The Granger Collection, New York. 7: (br) SuperStock; (tr) Tom Grill/CORBIS. 8: (t) Joe Raedle/Getty Images. 9: (c) SuperStock. 10: (bkgd) AP Photo/John Duricka. 11: (bc) Reuters/CORBIS; (bl) Mike Theiler/Getty Images; (br) Matthew Cavanaugh/epa/CORBIS. 12: (br) Torsten Leukert/vario images GmbH & Co.KG/Alamy Images; (t) Sygma/CORBIS. 13: (t) Jim Young/Reuters/Landov. 14: (b) Ken Heinen, Supreme Court/AP Photos. 15: (c) Matthew Cavanaugh/epa/CORBIS; (tr) C. Sherburne/Getty Images. 16: (cl) Susan Hestir/Gibbs Magnet School of International Studies and Foreign Languages. 17: (cr) Susan Hestir/Gibbs Magnet School of International Studies and Foreign Languages; (tl) Susan Hestir/Gibbs Magnet School of International Studies and Foreign Languages. 18: Walter Bibikow/Getty Images. 19: (b) Todd Gipstein/CORBIS. 20: (b) SuperStock. 22: (bl) Ed Pritchard/Getty Images. 22-23: (b) CORBIS. 23: (c) Super-Stock; (r) Henryk Kaiser/Index Stock Imagery. 24: Barry Winiker/Index Stock Imagery. 25: (b) Cathy Melloan Resources/PhotoEdit. 26: (br) Jeremy Walker/Getty Images; (tr) Marilyn Humphries/The Image Works, Inc. 27: (t) Supreme Court of Ohio. 28: (b) Andrew J. Martinez/Photo Researchers, Inc.; (bl) Joe Sohm/Visions of America, LLC/Alamy Images. 29: (c) Barry Winiker/Index Stock Imagery; (tr) Tom Tietz/Getty Images. 32: Orlin Wagner/AP Photos. 33: (b) Cliff Schiappa/AP Photos. 34: (cr) City of Kansas City, MO; (t) City of Kansas City, MO. 35: (c) Cliff Schiappa/AP Photos. 36: Jupiterimages. 37: (br) C Squared Studios/Getty Images. 38: (br) Jonathon Nourok/PhotoEdit; (tc) Lewis Hine/The Granger Collection, New York; (tl) G. Krishnan/Bruce Coleman Inc.; (tr) 2005 Roger-Viollet/The Image Works, Inc. 39: (c) Paul Richards/AFP/Getty Images. 40: (c) Hulton Archive/Getty Images; (cr) Museum of London/Topham-HIP/The Image Works, Inc. 41: (bl) Social History Division/Smithsonian Institution, National Museum of American History; (br) Minnesota Historical Society/CORBIS; (tl) Library of Congress, Prints & Photographs Division, LC-USZ61-791; (tr) Museum of London / Topham-HIP/The Image Works, Inc. 42: (br) AP Photos; (br) Bettmann Archive/CORBIS. 43: (c) Paul Richards/Getty Images. 46: (br) Ken Karp for MMH; (tr) Ken Karp for MMH. R1: (br) Andre Jenny/Alamy Images; (cr) Jim Young/Reuters/Landov; (tr) Cathy Melloan Resources/PhotoEdit; (tr) William S Helsel/Getty Images. R2: (br) Marilyn Humphries/The Image Works, Inc.; (br) Lewis Hine/The Granger Collection, New York; (cr) Pool/Getty Images; (tl) Joe Raedle/Getty Images. R3: (br) CORBIS; (br) Tom Brakefield/Getty Images; (cr) Orlin Wagner/AP Photos; (tr) Hulton Archive/Getty Images; (tr) Matthew Cavanaugh/epa/CORBIS.